Contents

Phonics Centers

Level B

What's Great About This Book

Centers are a wonderful, fun way for students to practice important skills. The 13 centers in this book are self-contained and portable. Students may work at a table or even on the floor. Once you've made the centers, they're ready to use at any time.

Everything You Need

- Teacher direction page

    How to make the center

    Description of student task

- Full-color materials needed for the center
- Reproducible student activity sheets

Using the Center

The centers are intended for skill practice, not to introduce skills. It is important to model the use of each center before students do the task independently.

Questions to Consider

- Will students select a center, or will you assign the center?
- Will there be a specific block of time for centers, or will the centers be used throughout the day?
- Where will you place the centers for easy access by students?
- What procedure will students use when they need help with the center tasks?
- Where will students store completed work?
- How will you track the tasks and centers completed by each student?

Making an Envelope Center

Materials

- 9" x 12" (23 x 30.5 cm) large envelopes
- scissors
- marking pens
- glue or two-sided tape

Steps to Follow

1. Remove and laminate the center cover page. Glue or tape it to the front of the envelope.

2. Remove and laminate the student direction page. Glue or tape it to the back of the envelope.

3. Remove, laminate, and cut apart the manipulatives (sorting mats, task cards, pockets, etc.) and place them in the envelope.

4. Reproduce the student activity sheet and place copies in the envelope.

Note: If a center contains small pieces such as letter cards, place them in a smaller envelope within the larger envelope.

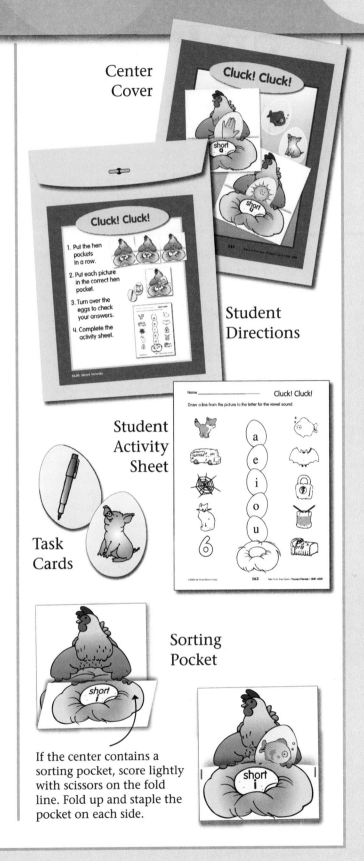

Center Cover

Student Directions

Student Activity Sheet

Task Cards

Sorting Pocket

If the center contains a sorting pocket, score lightly with scissors on the fold line. Fold up and staple the pocket on each side.

Pair Them Up Puzzles

Skill: Visual Discrimination

Preparing the Center

1. Prepare an envelope following the directions on page 3.
   - Cover—page 5
   - Student Directions—page 7
   - Task Cards—pages 9–17
2. Reproduce a supply of the student activity sheet on page 19.
3. Place all center materials in the envelope.

Using the Center

In a Small Group

Place all cards faceup on a flat surface. Students take turns choosing a puzzle piece. They find a second puzzle piece to make a match. Continue play until all cards have been matched.

Independently

The student matches two cards at a time to complete a puzzle. Then the student circles the words on the activity sheet to show that they are the same.

Self-Checking Key

Matching cards have the same colored design on the back.

Pair Them Up Puzzles

see   see

can   that

I love puzzles!

5

6

Pair Them Up Puzzles

1. Find the cards that are the same.

2. Put them together.

3. Turn over the cards to check your answers.

4. Complete the activity sheet.

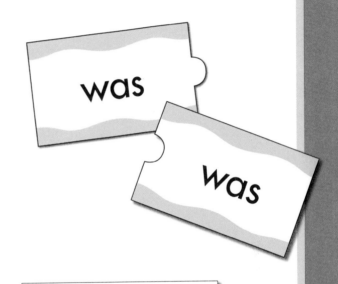

Name _____

Circle the two words that are the same.

Pair Them Up
Puzzles

1.	at	at	an
2.	see	bee	see
3.	up	pup	pup
4.	the	he	the
5.	no	not	no
6.	can	an	an
7.	it	in	it
8.	was	was	saw
9.	run	ran	ran

©2004 by Evan-Moor Corp. 19 Take It to Your Seat—Phonics Centers • EMC 3328

Skill: Visual Discrimination

8

it

it

in

in

on

on

can

can

was

was

saw

saw

up

up

pup

pup

11

run

run

ran

ran

he

he

be

be

at

at

an

an

see

see

bee

bee

Take It to Your Seat—Phonics Centers • EMC 3328

that

that

the

the

no

no

not

not

Name _____

Circle the two words that are the same.

1.	at	at	an
2.	see	bee	see
3.	up	pup	pup
4.	the	he	the
5.	no	not	no
6.	can	an	an
7.	it	in	it
8.	was	was	saw
9.	run	ran	ran

Rhymes Go Round

Skill: Rhyming Words

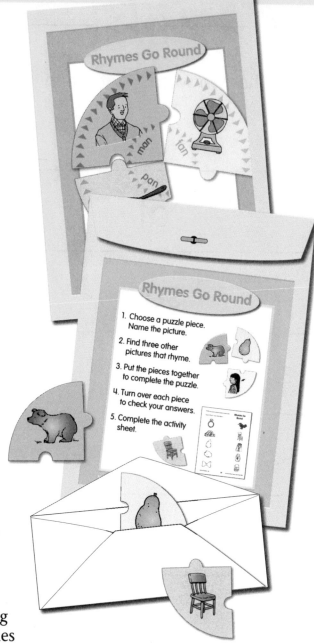

Preparing the Center

1. Prepare an envelope following the directions on page 3.
   Cover—page 21
   Student Directions—page 23
   Task Cards—pages 25–31
2. Reproduce a supply of the student activity sheet on page 33.
3. Place all center materials in the envelope.

Using the Center

In a Small Group

Spread out the puzzle pieces faceup on a flat surface. Have students take turns choosing and naming a puzzle piece, listening for the rhyming words. Students put the four rhyming pieces together to complete each circle.

Independently

The student forms eight sets of rhyming picture circles. Then the student matches pairs of rhyming objects on the activity sheet.

Self-Checking Key

Turn over each set of four pieces. The back of each matching puzzle piece is the same color and has the same shape on it.

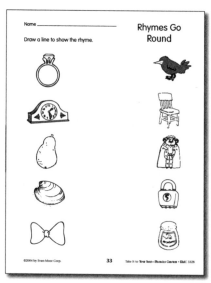

Rhymes Go Round

man

fan

pan

Take It to Your Seat—Phonics Centers • EMC 3328

Rhymes Go Round

1. Choose a puzzle piece. Name the picture.

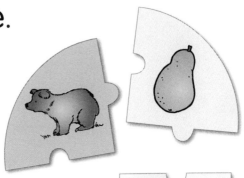

2. Find three other pictures that rhyme.

3. Put the pieces together to complete the puzzle.

4. Turn over each piece to check your answers.

5. Complete the activity sheet.

Skill: Rhyming Words

24

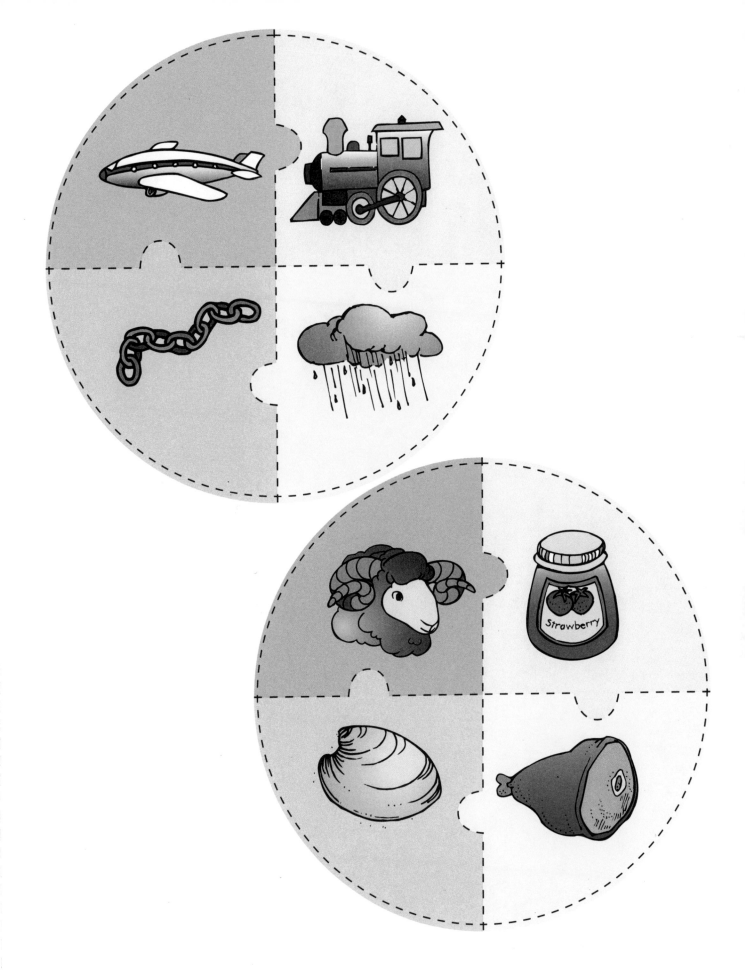

©2004 by Evan-Moor Corp.
Take It to Your Seat—
Phonics Centers
EMC 3328

©2004 by Evan-Moor Corp.
Take It to Your Seat—
Phonics Centers
EMC 3328

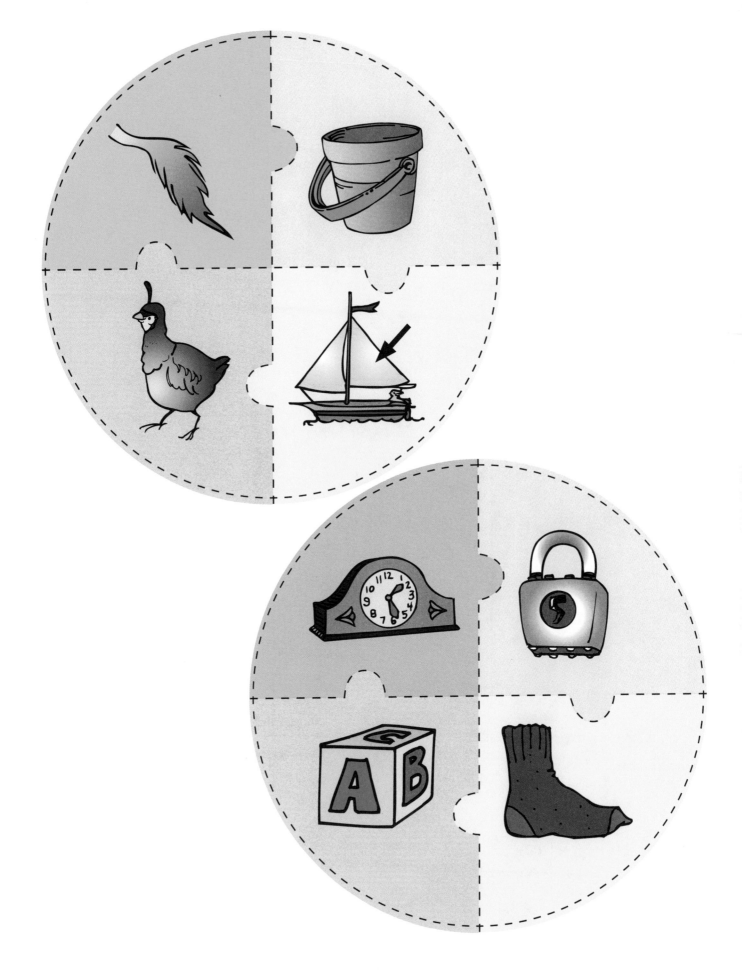

©2004 by Evan-Moor Corp.
Take It to Your Seat—
Phonics Centers
EMC 3328

©2004 by Evan-Moor Corp.
Take It to Your Seat—
Phonics Centers
EMC 3328

28

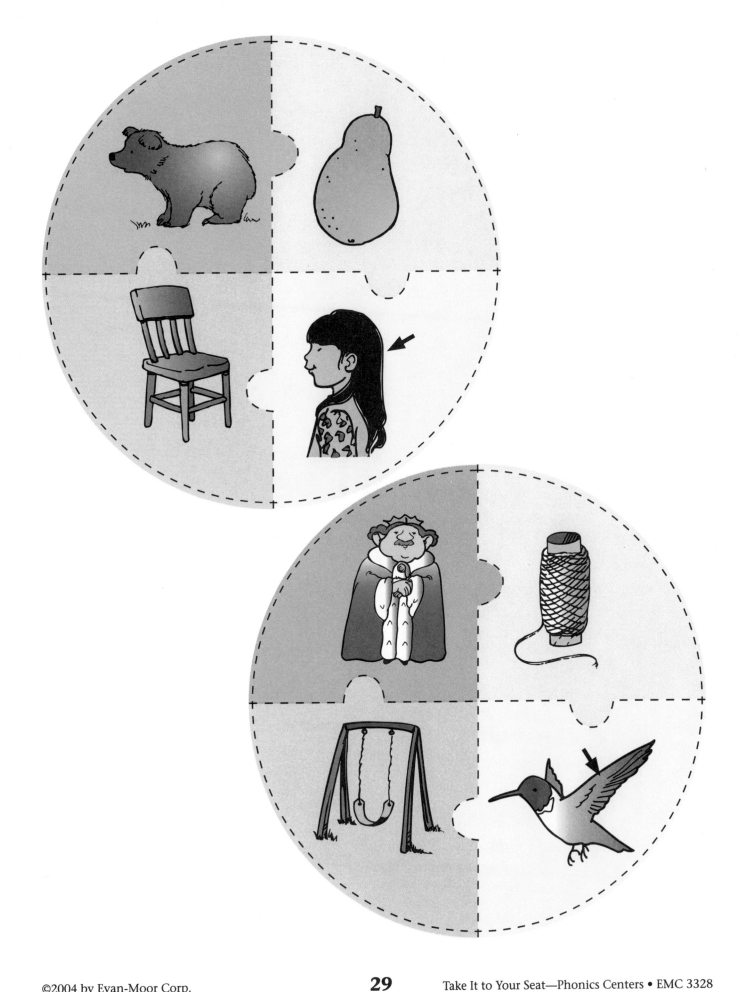

©2004 by Evan-Moor Corp.
Take It to Your Seat—
Phonics Centers
EMC 3328

©2004 by Evan-Moor Corp.
Take It to Your Seat—
Phonics Centers
EMC 3328

Name _____

Draw a line to show the rhyme.

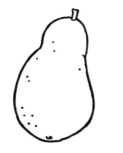

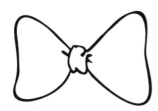

Ant Families

Skill: Word Families

Preparing the Center

1. Prepare an envelope following the directions on page 3.
   Cover—page 35
   Student Directions—page 37
   Sorting Pockets—pages 39 and 41
   Task Cards—pages 43 and 45
2. Reproduce a supply of the student activity sheet on page 47.
3. Place all center materials in the envelope.

Using the Center

In a Small Group
Lay the sorting pockets (anthills) faceup on a flat surface. Have students take turns choosing an ant card and placing it on the correct anthill. Ants are correctly placed when the word on the ant card is part of the word family on the anthill.

Independently
The student sorts and places the ant cards in the correct pocket. The student then writes the words on the correct anthill on the activity sheet.

Self-Checking Key
The matching word family pocket label and the back of the ant cards are the same color.

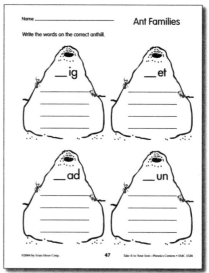

Ant Families

36

Ant Families

1. Match each ant to the correct hill.

2. Turn over the ant cards to check your answers.

3. Complete the activity sheet.

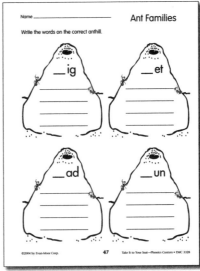

Skill: Word Families

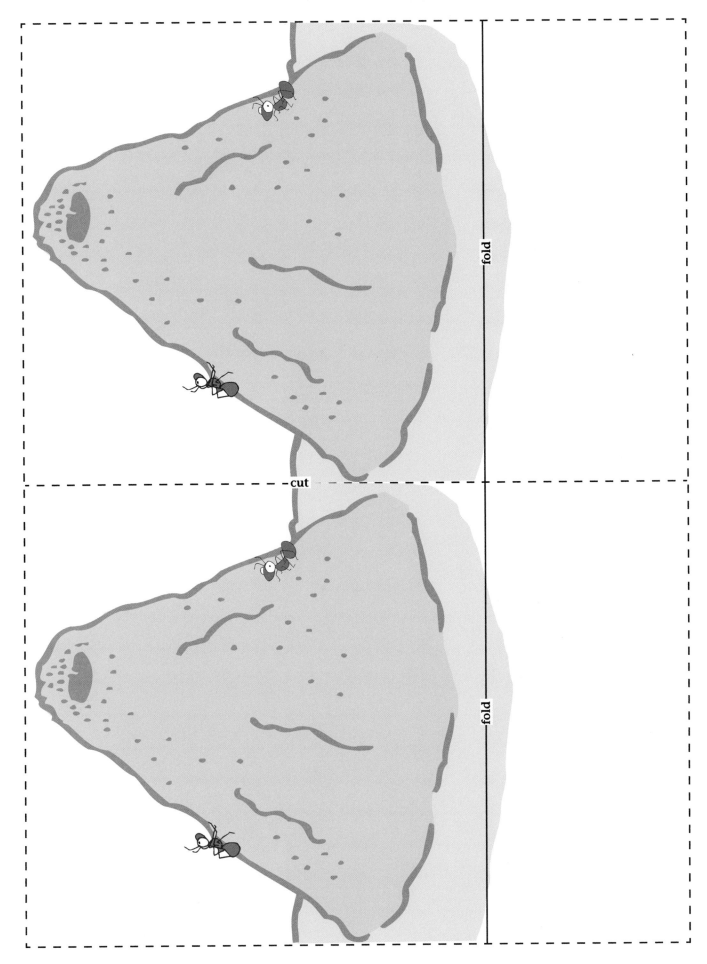

fold

cut

fold

Take It to Your Seat—Phonics Centers • EMC 3328

_ig

_et

fold

fold

40

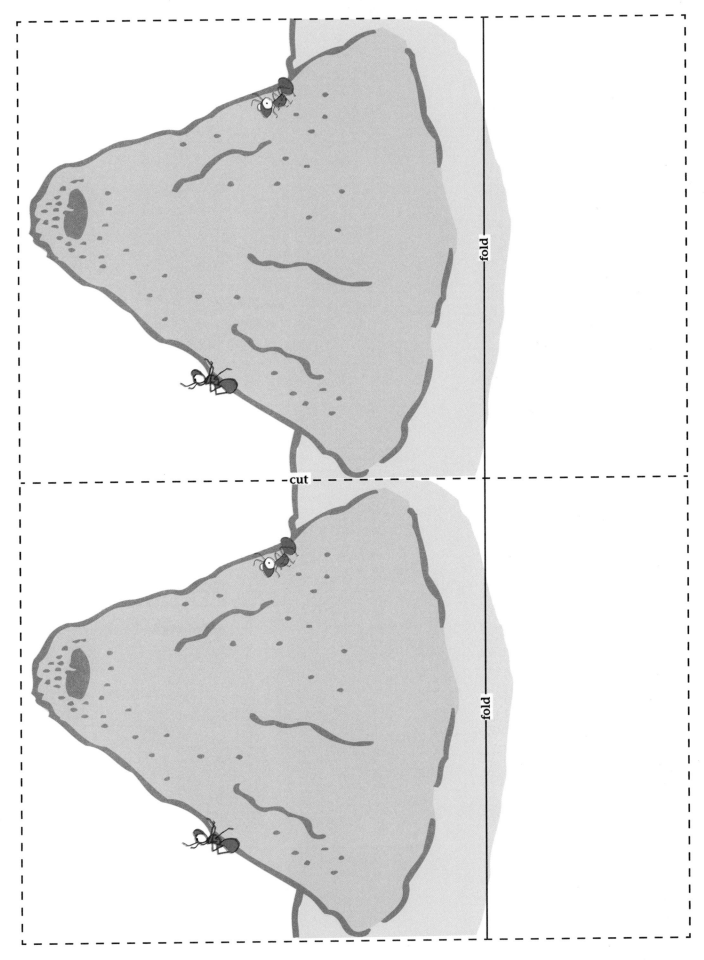

fold

cut

fold

41

_ad

_un

fold

fold

42

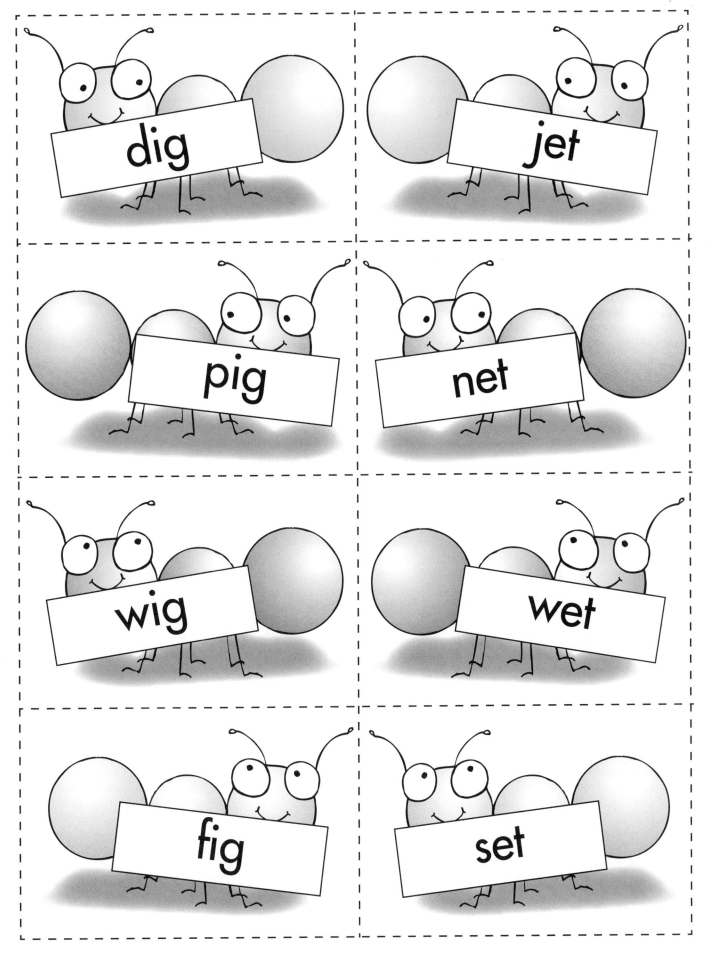

dig

jet

pig

net

wig

wet

fig

set

dad

sun

sad

bun

mad

fun

had

run

Name _____

Write the words on the correct anthill.

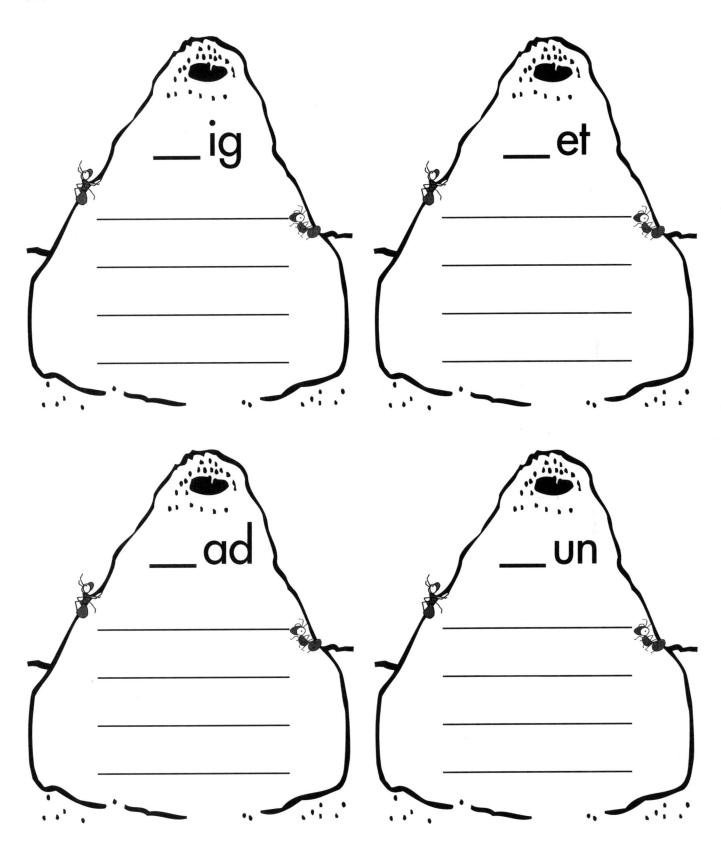

_ig

_et

_ad

_un

Cookie Sort

Skill: Word Families

Preparing the Center

1. Prepare an envelope following the directions on page 3.
   Cover—page 49
   Student Directions—page 51
   Sorting Pockets—pages 53 and 55
   Task Cards—pages 57 and 59
2. Reproduce a supply of the student activity sheet on page 61.
3. Place all center materials in the envelope.

Using the Center

In a Small Group

Lay the cookie cards and cookie jars faceup on a flat surface. One at a time, students choose a cookie, read the word, and place the cookie on the correct cookie jar. Continue until all cookies have been placed.

Independently

The student lines up the cookie jars. Then the student reads the words and matches the cookies to each cookie jar. Finally, the student writes the words in the correct cookie jar on the activity sheet.

Self-Checking Key

The back of each cookie and its matching cookie jar have the same colored shape.

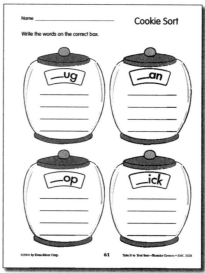

Cookie Sort

50

Cookie Sort

1. Match the cookies to the correct cookie jar.

2. Turn over the cookies to check your answers.

3. Write the words on the cookies in the correct cookie jar on the activity sheet.

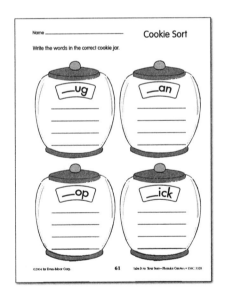

Skill: Word Families

fold

cut

fold

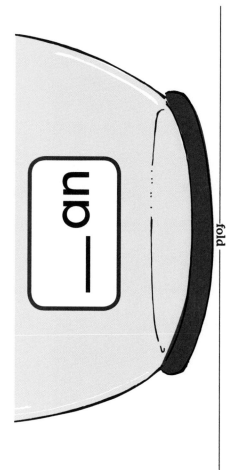

un —

fold

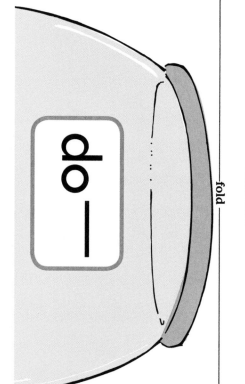

do —

fold

54

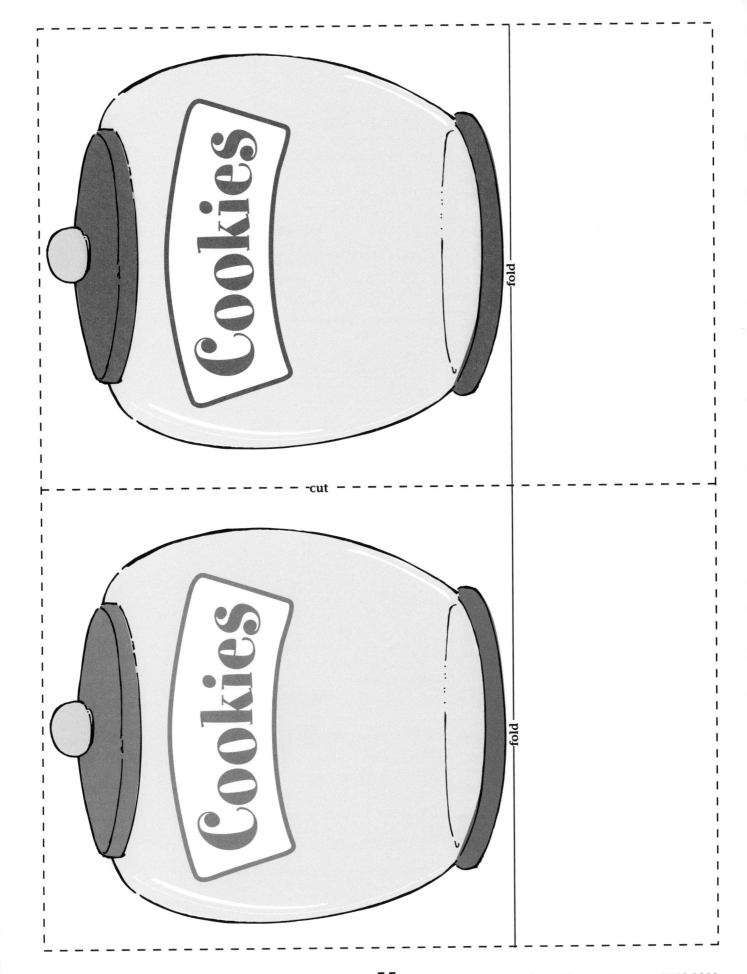

cut

fold

fold

55

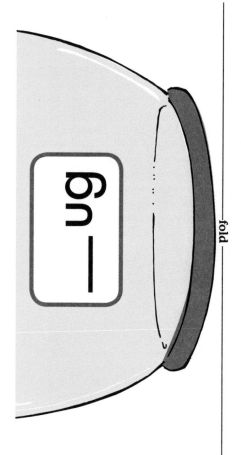

—ug

©2004 by Evan-Moor Corp.
Take It to Your Seat—Phonics Centers
EMC 3328

fold

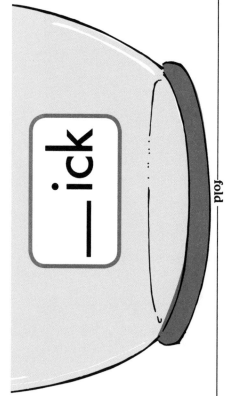

—ick

fold

56

hop

man

mop

fan

stop

pan

top

ran

57

58

mug

sick

rug

kick

hug

stick

bug

chick

59

Write the words in the correct cookie jar.

_ug

_an

_op

_ick

Bunch of Balloons

Skill: Word Families

Preparing the Center

1. Prepare an envelope following the directions on page 3.
   - Cover—page 63
   - Student Directions—page 65
   - Sorting Pockets—pages 67 and 69
   - Task Cards—pages 71 and 73
2. Reproduce a supply of the student activity sheet on page 75.
3. Place all center materials in the envelope.

Using the Center

In a Small Group

Lay the balloon cards and sorting mats faceup on a flat surface. One at a time, students choose a balloon, read the word, and then match the balloon to the correct bunch of balloons. Continue until all balloons have been placed.

Independently

The student lines up the sorting mats. Then the student reads the words and matches the balloons to the correct "bunch." Finally, the student writes the words in the correct balloon on the activity sheet.

Self-Checking Key

The back of each balloon and its matching sorting mat have the same colored shape.

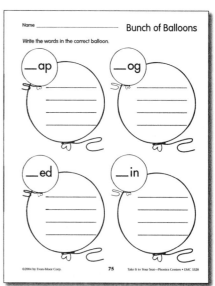

Bunch of Balloons

Bunch of Balloons

1. Match the balloons to the correct mat.

2. Turn over the balloons to check your answers.

3. Write the words in the correct balloon on the activity sheet.

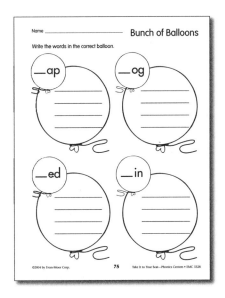

Skill: Word Families

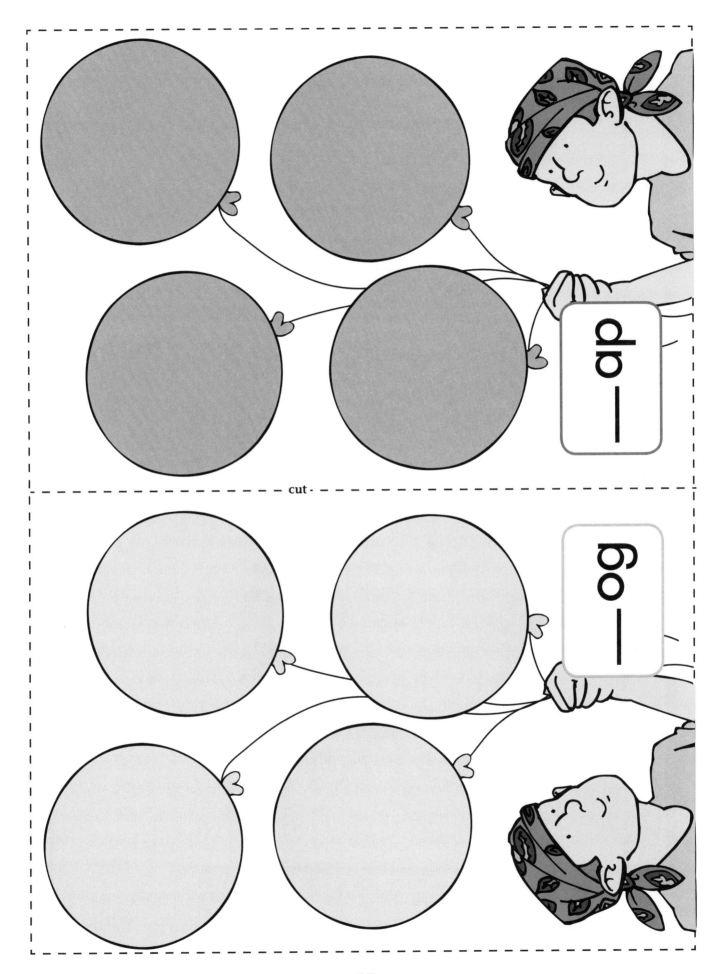

68

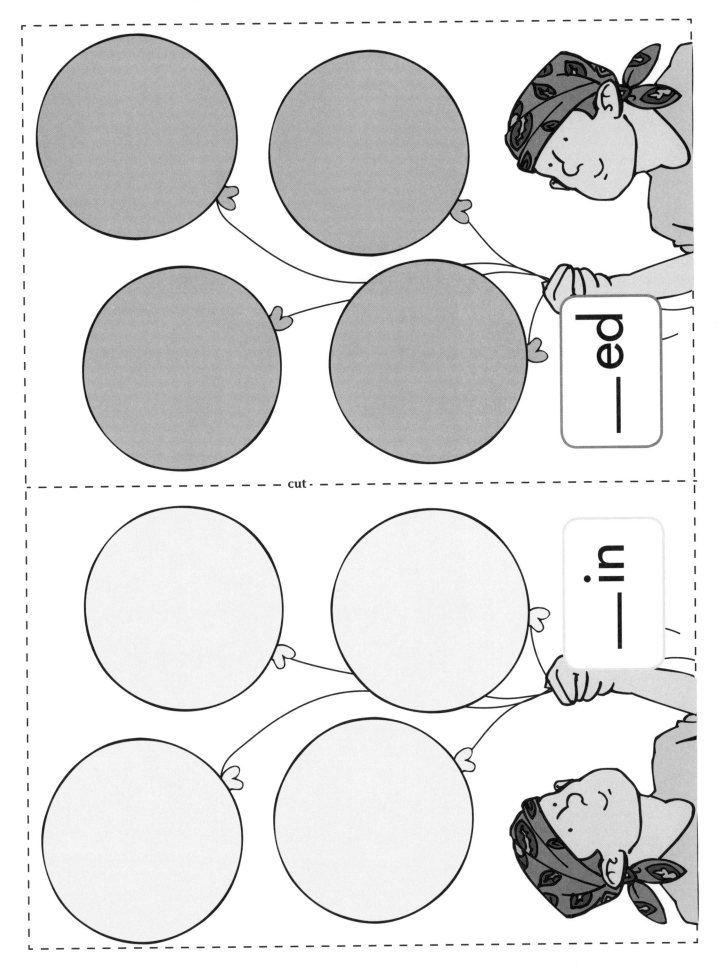

69

70

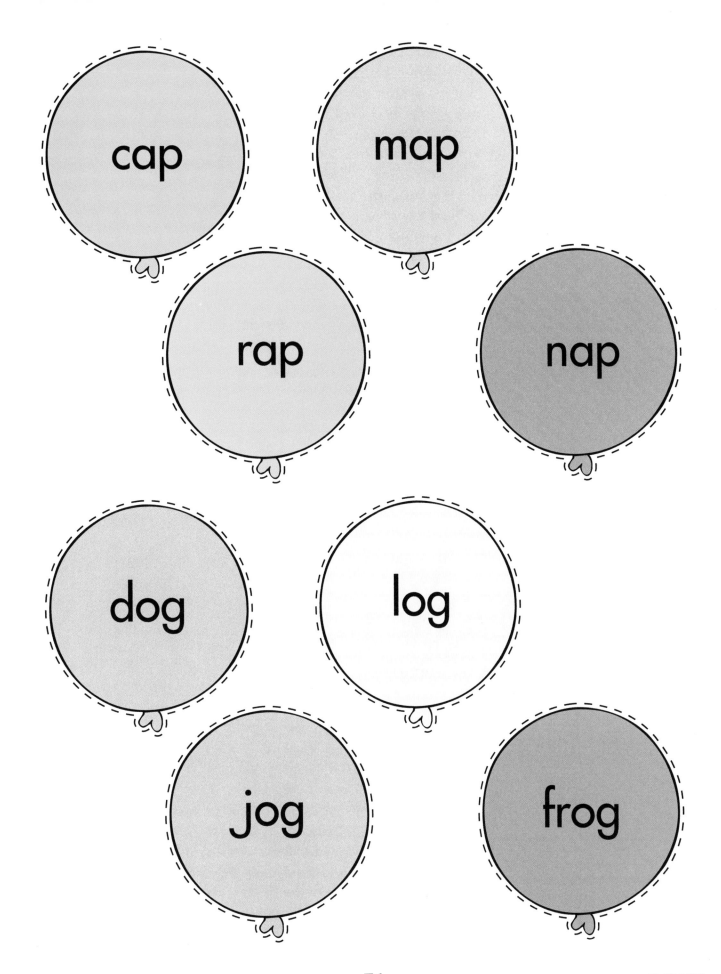

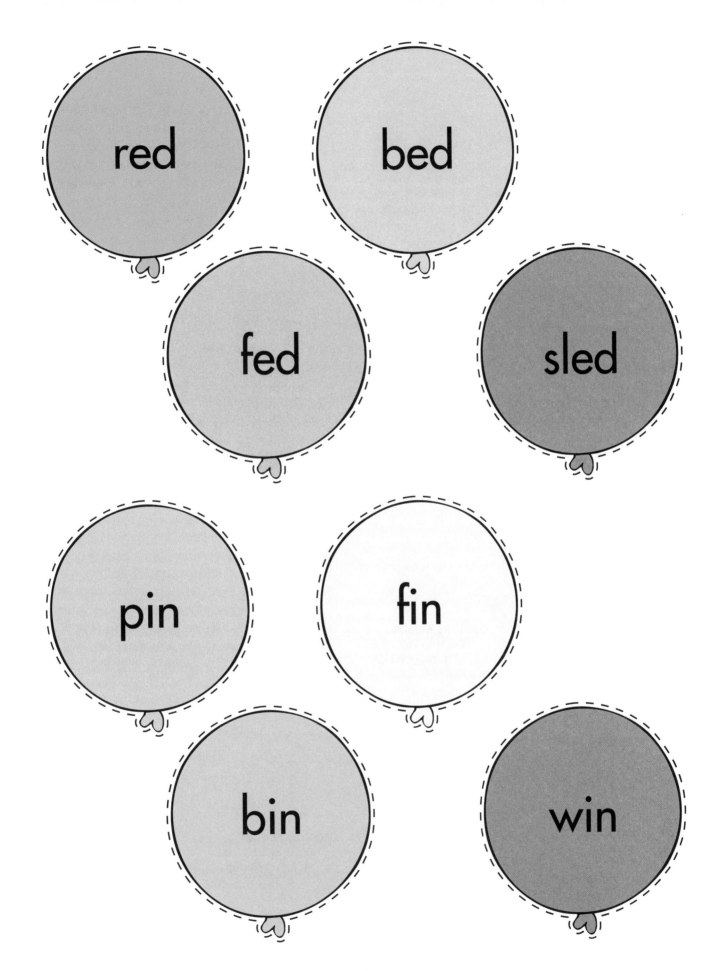

red

bed

fed

sled

pin

fin

bin

win

Take It to Your Seat—Phonics Centers • EMC 3328

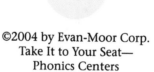

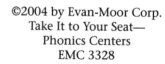

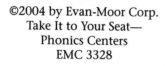

Name _____

Bunch of Balloons

Write the words in the correct balloon.

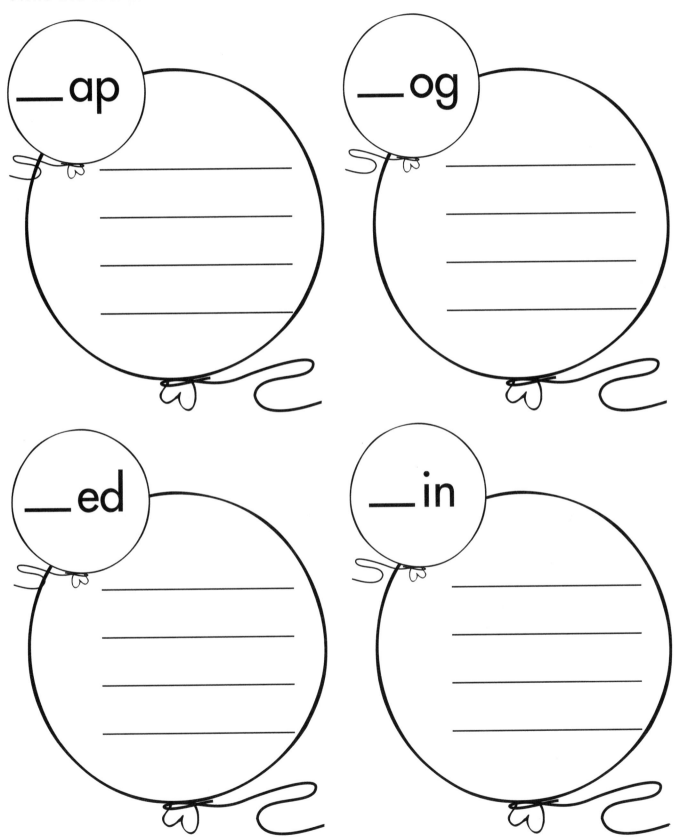

All Aboard the ABC Train

Skill: Matching Upper- and Lowercase Letters

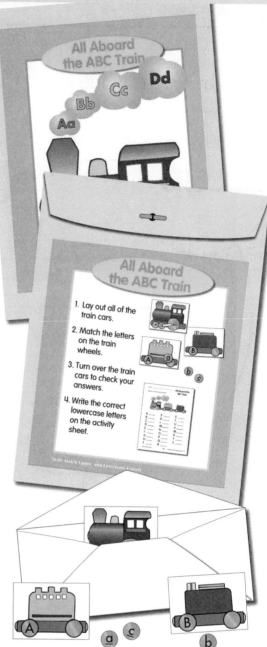

Preparing the Center

1. Prepare an envelope following the directions on page 3.
   - Cover—page 77
   - Student Directions—page 79
   - Task Cards—pages 81–89
2. Reproduce a supply of the student activity sheet on page 91.
3. Place all center materials in the envelope.

Using the Center

In a Small Group

Place the train engine and cars faceup on a flat surface. Place the train wheels in a small bag or box. One student at a time selects a wheel and matches it to the capital letter on a train car. Continue taking turns until all letters have been matched.

The lesson may be extended by having students place the train cars in alphabetical order.

Independently

The student matches the lowercase train wheels to the correct uppercase wheel. Then the student writes the correct lowercase letters on the activity sheet.

Extend the lesson by having the student place the train cars in alphabetical order.

Self-Checking Key

Cards have the correct upper- and lowercase letters on the back.

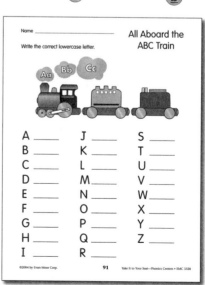

77

78

All Aboard the ABC Train

1. Lay out all of the train cars.

2. Match the letters on the train wheels.

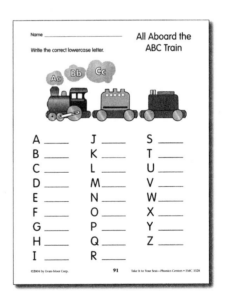

3. Turn over the train cars to check your answers.

4. Write the correct lowercase letters on the activity sheet.

Skill: Matching Upper- and Lowercase Letters

80

All Aboard!
the ABC Train

Bb

Aa

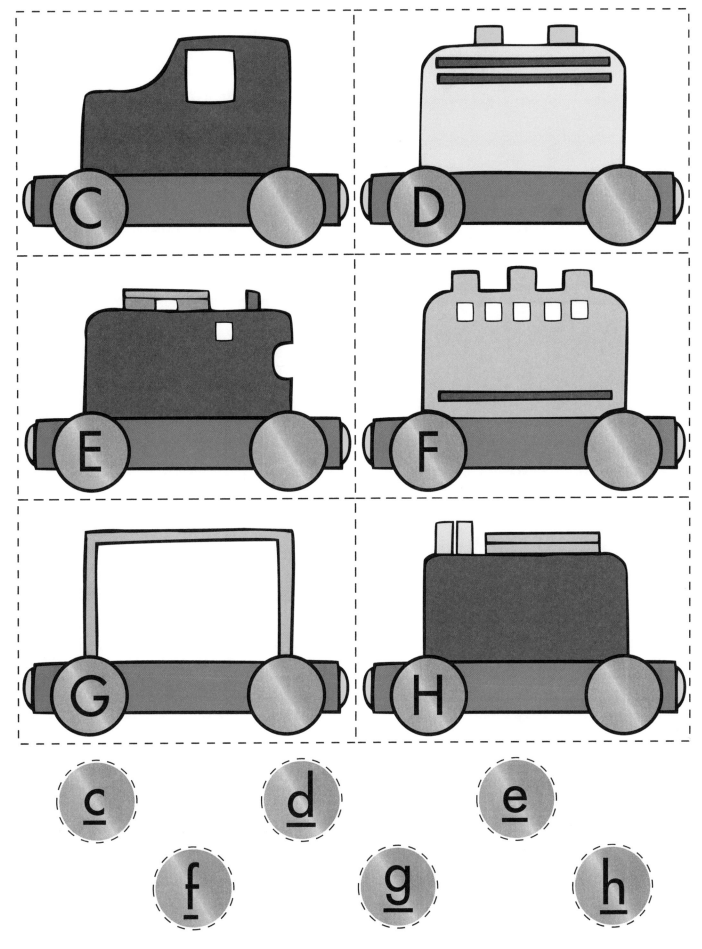

Dd

Cc

Ff

Ee

Hh

Gg

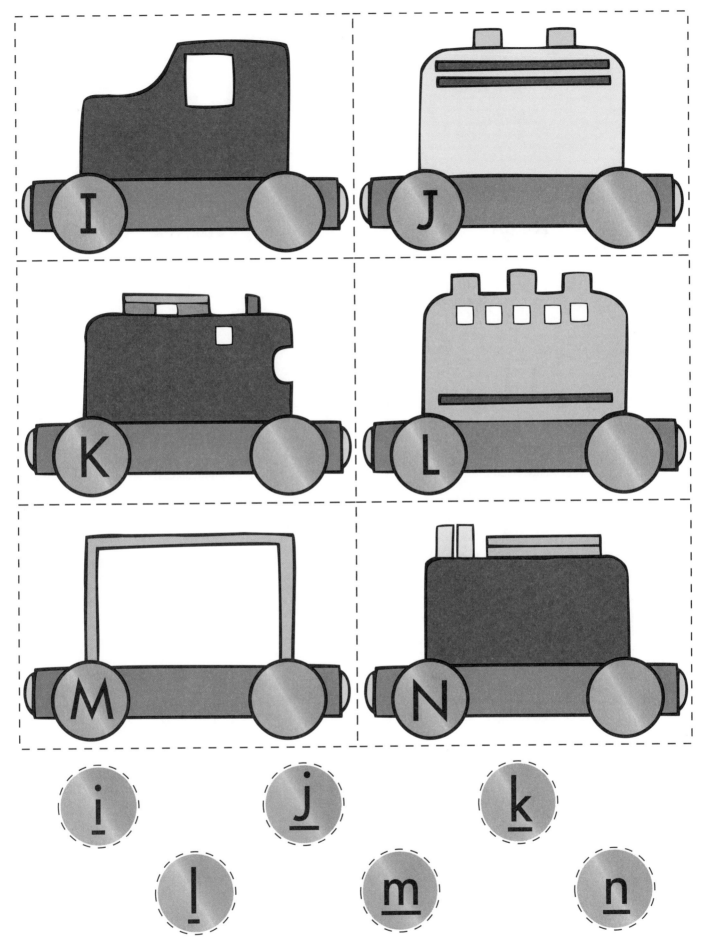

Jj

Ii

Ll

Kk

Nn

Mm

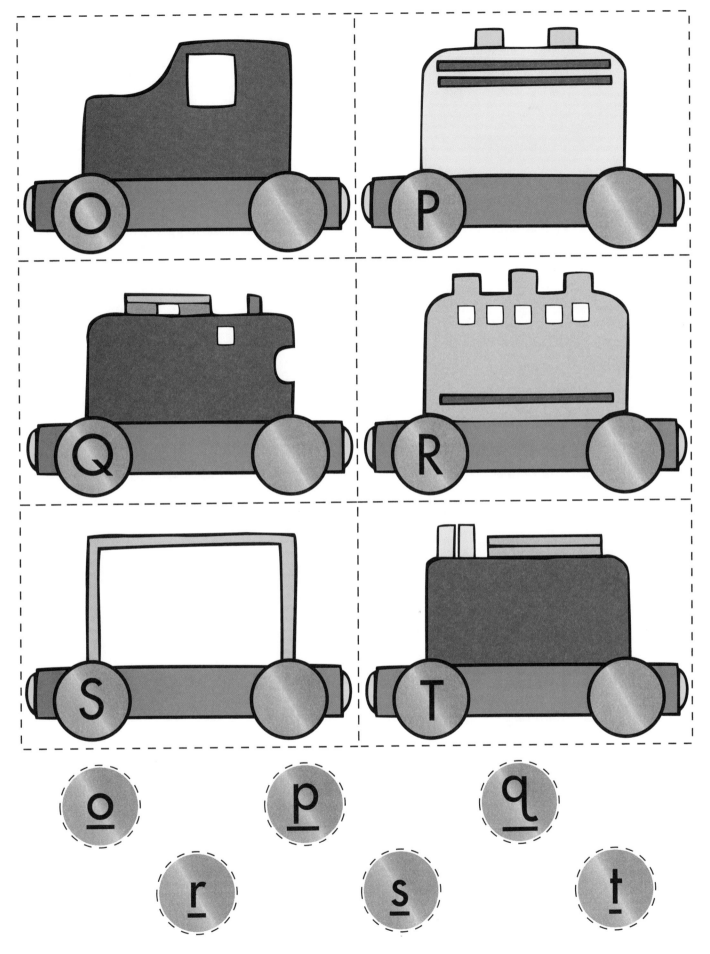

Pp

Oo

Rr

Qq

Tt

Ss

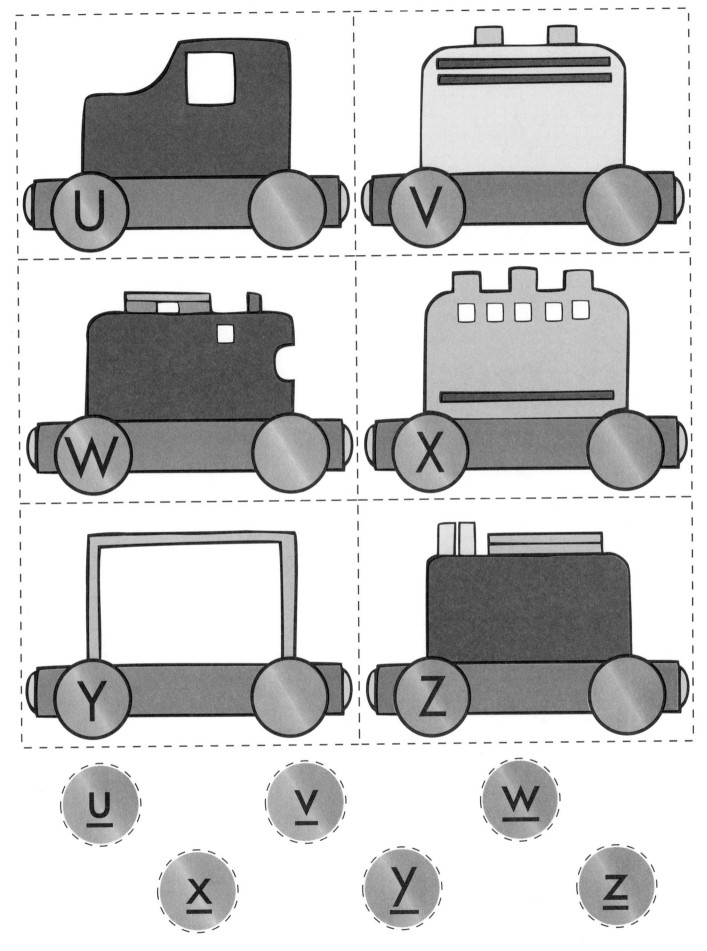

Vv

Uu

Xx

Ww

Zz

Yy

Name _____

All Aboard the
ABC Train

Write the correct lowercase letter.

A _____ J _____ S _____

B _____ K _____ T _____

C _____ L _____ U _____

D _____ M _____ V _____

E _____ N _____ W _____

F _____ O _____ X _____

G _____ P _____ Y _____

H _____ Q _____ Z _____

I _____ R _____

©2004 by Evan-Moor Corp.

91

Take It to Your Seat—Phonics Centers • EMC 3328

Beginning Sounds

Skill: Listening for Initial Consonant Sounds: *b, c, f, h, j, l, n, p, r, z*

Preparing the Center

1. Prepare an envelope following the directions on page 3.
   - Cover—page 93
   - Student Directions—page 95
   - Task Cards—pages 97 and 99
2. Reproduce a supply of the student activity sheet on page 101.
3. Place all center materials in the envelope.

Using the Center

In a Small Group

Lay the letter strips on a flat surface. Hold up a letter strip and point to a letter. Students find the two pictures whose names begin with that sound. Students name each of the pictures, listen for the beginning sound, and then place the picture cards next to the correct letter.

Independently

The student lays the letter strips on a flat surface. The student selects a picture card and names the picture. Then the student places the card beside the letter that stands for the sound that is heard at the beginning of the word. The student makes two matches for each sound. On the activity sheet, the student draws one picture for each given letter.

Self-Checking Key

Turn over each pair of picture cards. The correct initial consonant is on the back of each card.

Beginning Sounds

C
Cat

B
boy

F
fun!

Beginning Sounds

1. Lay out the letter strips.

2. Choose a picture. Say the name.

3. Listen for the beginning sound. Put the card next to the correct letter.

4. Match all the pictures to the correct letters.

5. Turn over the pictures to check your answers.

6. Complete the activity sheet.

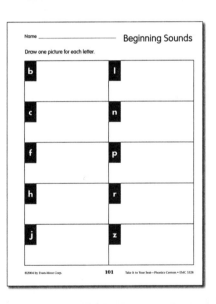

Skill: Listening for Initial Consonant Sounds: *b, c, f, h, j, l, n, p, r, z*

96

b

b

©2004 by Evan-Moor Corp.
Take It to Your Seat—Phonics Centers
EMC 3328

c

©2004 by Evan-Moor Corp.
Take It to Your Seat—Phonics Centers
EMC 3328

c

©2004 by Evan-Moor Corp.
Take It to Your Seat—Phonics Centers
EMC 3328

f

©2004 by Evan-Moor Corp.
Take It to Your Seat—Phonics Centers
EMC 3328

f

©2004 by Evan-Moor Corp.
Take It to Your Seat—Phonics Centers
EMC 3328

h

©2004 by Evan-Moor Corp.
Take It to Your Seat—Phonics Centers
EMC 3328

h

©2004 by Evan-Moor Corp.
Take It to Your Seat—Phonics Centers
EMC 3328

j

©2004 by Evan-Moor Corp.
Take It to Your Seat—Phonics Centers
EMC 3328

j

©2004 by Evan-Moor Corp.
Take It to Your Seat—Phonics Centers
EMC 3328

l

l

n

n

p

p

r

r

z

z

Beginning Sounds

Draw one picture for each letter.

b	**l**
c	**n**
f	**p**
h	**r**
j	**z**

101

Flower Garden

Skill: Listening for Initial Consonant Sounds: *d, g, k, m, q, s, t, v, w, y*

Preparing the Center

1. Prepare an envelope following the directions on page 3.
   - Cover—page 103
   - Student Directions—page 105
   - Task Cards—pages 107–115
2. Reproduce a supply of the student activity sheet on page 117.
3. Place all center materials in the envelope.

Using the Center

In a Small Group
Lay the letter cards (flower centers) and picture cards (flower petals) on a flat surface. Hold up a letter card. Students find pictures whose names begin with the letter on the card. Students name each of the pictures, listen for the sound of the letter, and place the pictures (petals) around the correct letter (flower center). The four pictures with the same beginning sound form a flower with the letter in the center.

Independently
The student lays the letter cards on a flat surface. The student selects a picture card, names the picture, and places it by the letter that stands for the sound that is heard at the beginning of the word. The four picture cards are placed to form a flower with the letter in the center.

On the activity sheet, the student writes the letter for the beginning sound of each picture name.

Self-Checking Key
Turn over the five pieces in each flower. When grouped correctly, all of the pieces will be the same color and have the same letter on them.

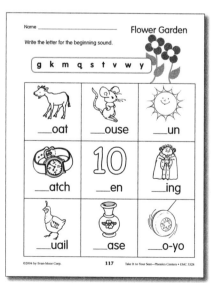

Flower Garden

k

d

m

104

Flower Garden

1. Name each picture. Put it on the flower center that has the same beginning sound.

2. Find three other cards that begin with the same sound to make a flower.

3. Make another flower.

4. Turn over all the flower pieces to check your answers.

5. Complete the activity sheet.

Skill: Listening for Initial Consonant Sounds: *d, g, k, m, q, s, t, v, w, y*

106

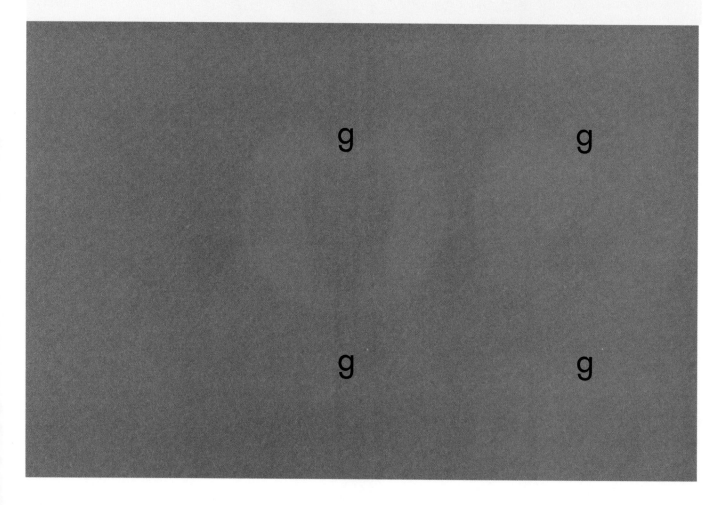

d   d

d   d

g   g

g   g

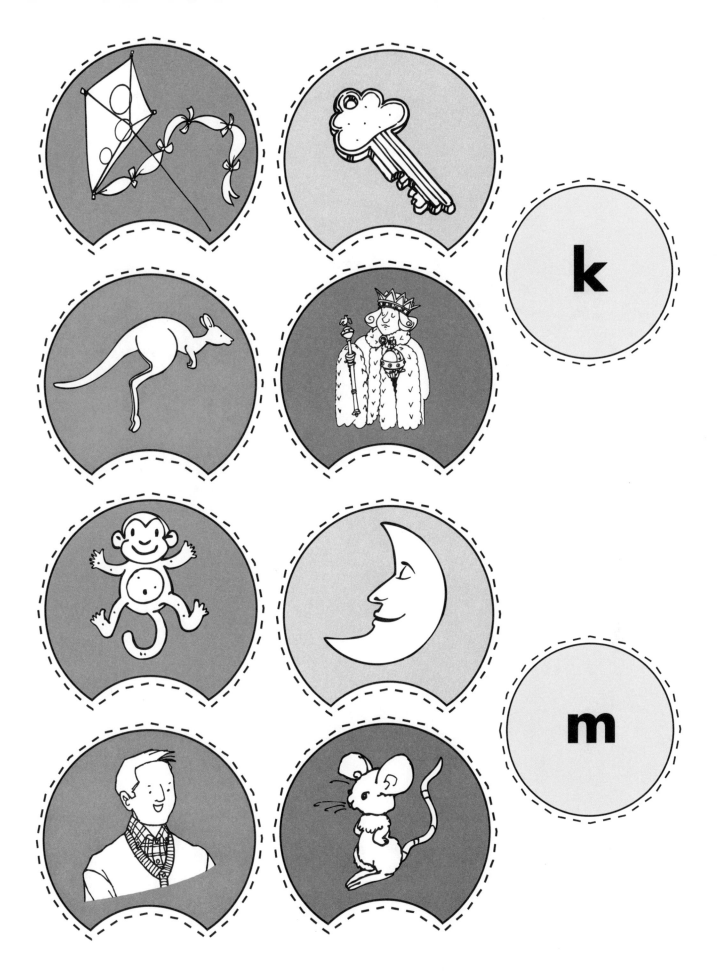

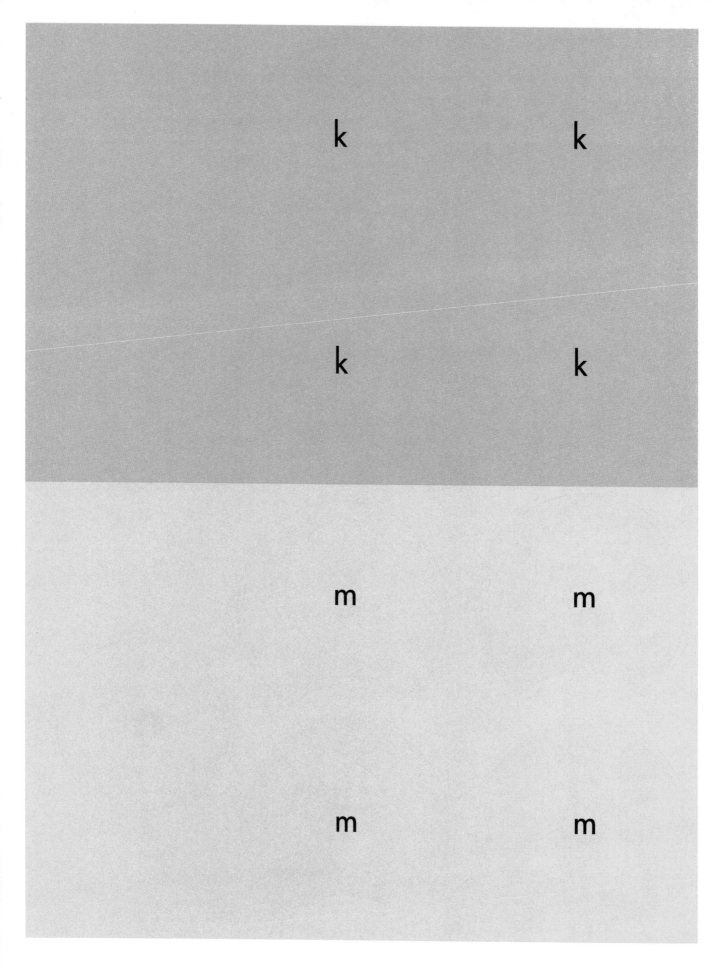

k   k

k   k

m   m

m   m

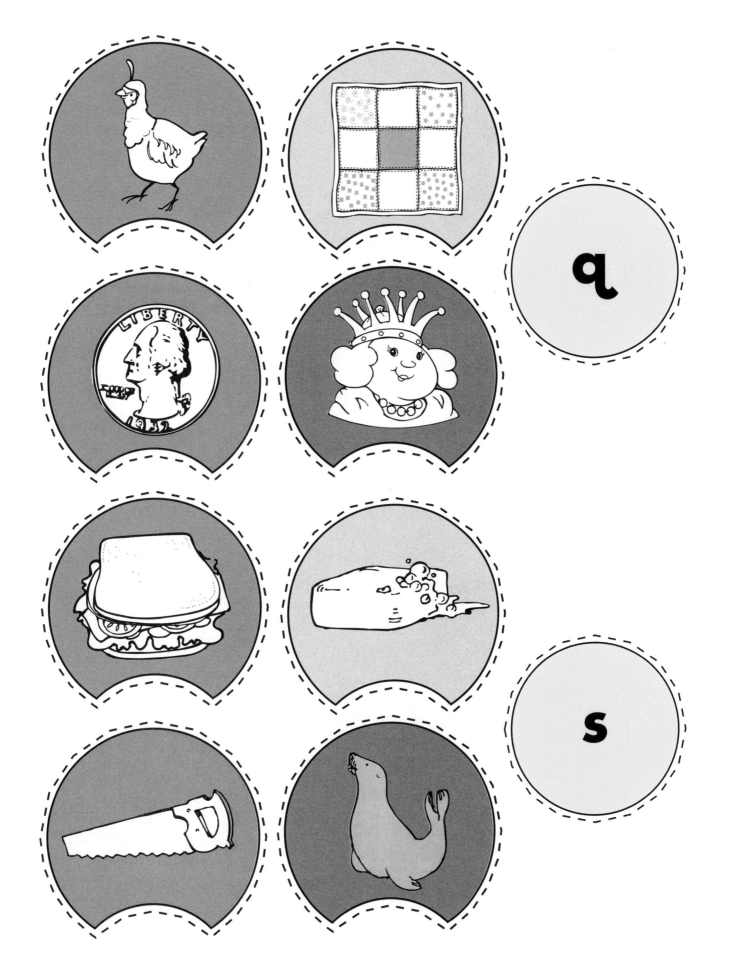

q q

q q

s s

s s

113

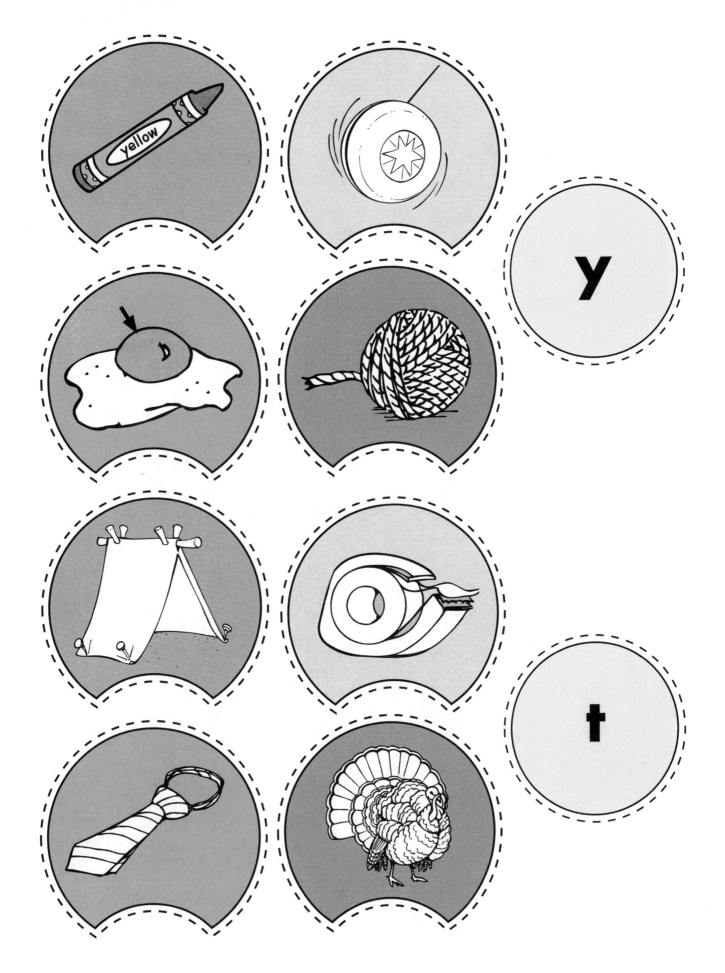

 Take It to Your Seat—Phonics Centers • EMC 3328

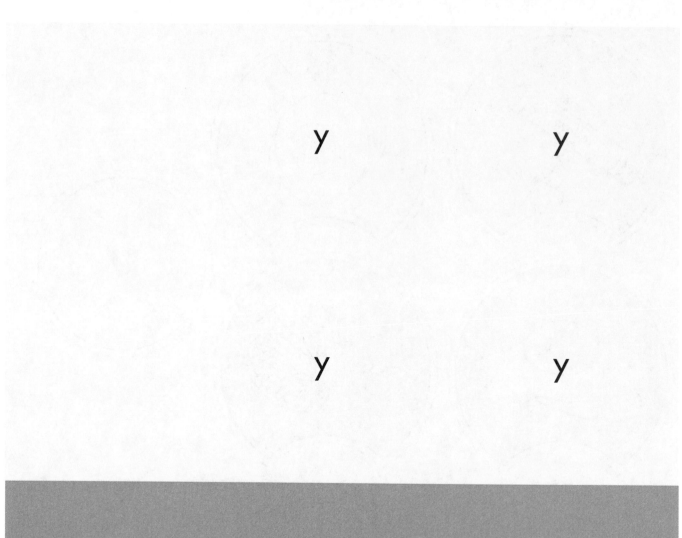

Name _____

Write the letter for the beginning sound.

| g | k | m | q | s | t | v | w | y |

___oat

___ouse

___un

___atch

___en

___ing

___uail

___ase

___o-yo

Take It to Your Seat—Phonics Centers • EMC 3328

What's at the End?

Skill: Listening for Final Consonant Sounds

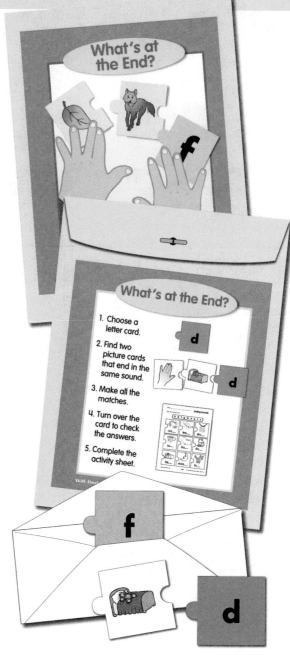

Preparing the Center

1. Prepare an envelope following the directions on page 3.
    Cover—page 119
    Student Directions—page 121
    Task Cards—pages 123–129
2. Reproduce a supply of the student activity sheet on page 131.
3. Place all center materials in the envelope.

Using the Center

In a Small Group

Ask students to listen for ending sounds. Students take turns choosing and naming picture cards. The two words with the same ending sound are placed together with the corresponding letter card.

Independently

The student forms pairs of picture cards with the same ending sound, and then matches them to their corresponding letter cards. Students write the correct ending sounds on the activity sheet.

Self-Checking Key

Each set of three puzzle pieces has the same colored design on the back.

What's at the End?

119

120

What's at the End?

1. Choose a letter card.

2. Find two picture cards that end in the same sound.

3. Make all the matches.

4. Turn over the cards to check your answers.

5. Complete the activity sheet.

Skill: Listening for Final Consonant Sounds

Name _____ What's at the End?

Write the ending sound.

| b   d   f   g   m   n   p   t   x |

cra___

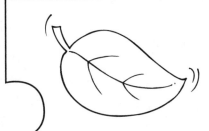

lea___

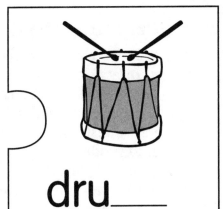

dru___

cu___

ba___

fro___

be___

moo___

fo___

Make a Word

Skill: Listening for Initial and Final Consonant Sounds

Preparing the Center

1. Prepare an envelope following the directions on page 3.
      Cover—page 133
      Student Directions—page 135
      Task Cards—pages 137–143
2. Reproduce a supply of the student activity sheet on page 145.
3. Place all center materials in the envelope.

Using the Center

In a Small Group

Lay the picture and letter cards on a flat surface. Hold up a picture card. Students name the picture and identify the initial sound they hear. They find the letter card for that sound and place it on the card. Next, they repeat the name of the picture, listen for the ending sound, and find the letter card for that sound. Continue the same process with the remaining picture cards.

Independently

The student uses the letter cards to place the beginning and ending sounds on each picture card. On the activity sheet, the student writes the missing letters to complete the word for each picture.

Self-Checking Key

The back of each card in a set contains the completed word.

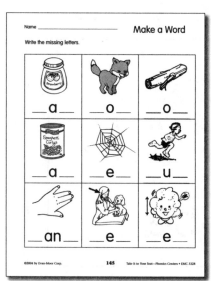

Make a Word

c a t

cat

r e

134

Make a Word

1. Name each picture.

2. Put the letter for the beginning sound on each card.

3. Put the letter for the ending sound on each card.

4. Turn over the cards to check your answers.

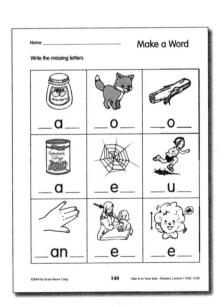

5. Complete the activity sheet.

Skill: Listening for Initial and Final Consonant Sounds

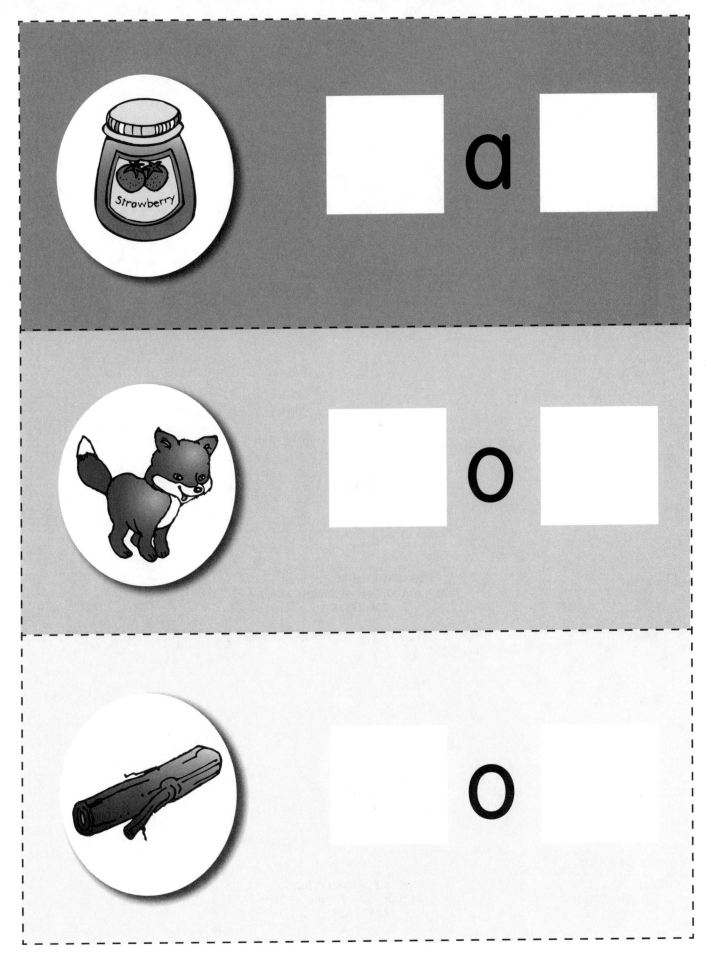

jam

fox

log

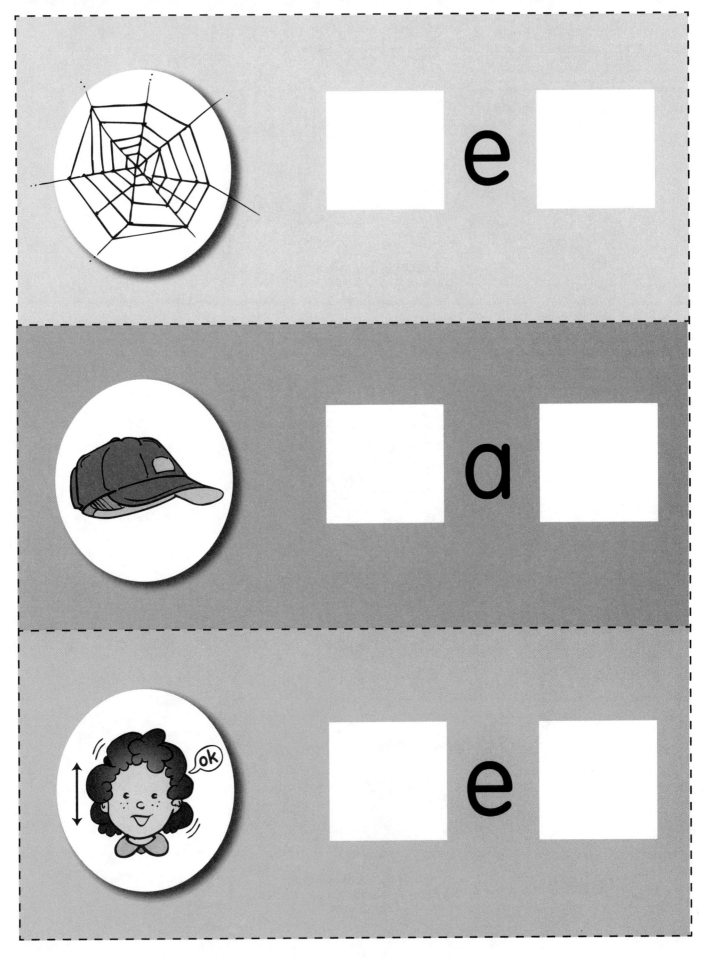

web

cap

yes

140

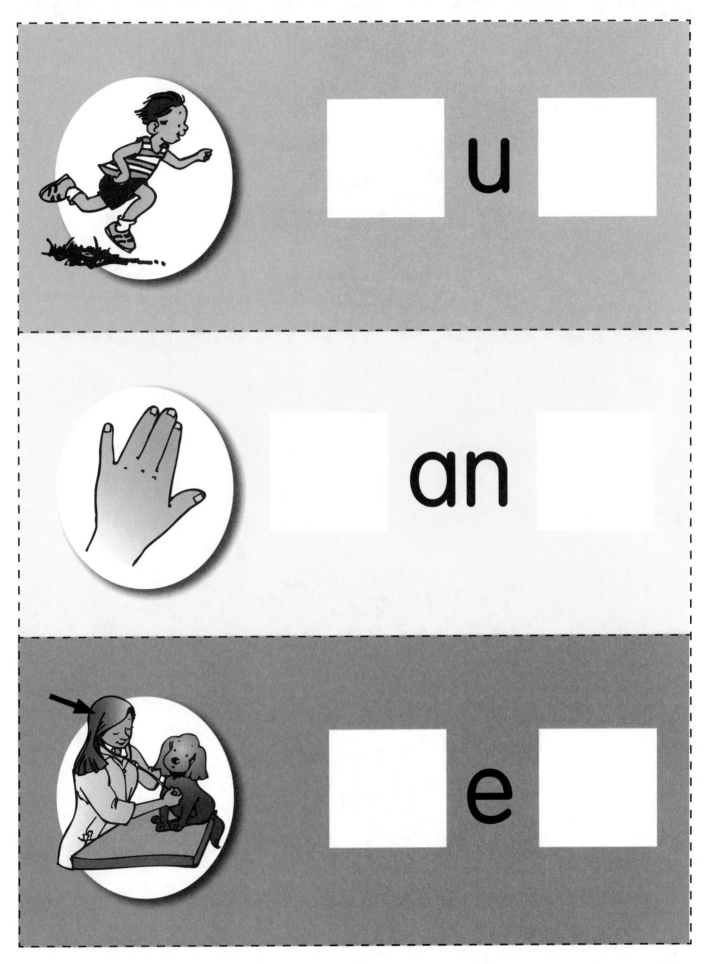

run

hand

vet

x	f	c	p	h
t	v	n	r	b
m	j	s	y	g
d	w	l		

143

h	p	c	f	x
hand	ca**p**	**c**ap	**f**ox	fo**x**

b	r	n	v	t
we**b**	**r**un	ru**n**	**v**et	ve**t**

g	y	s	j	m
lo**g**	**y**es	ye**s**	**j**am	ja**m**

l	w	d
log	**w**eb	han**d**

Make a Word

Write the missing letters.

 __ a __	 __ o __	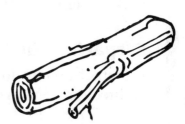 __ o __
 __ a __	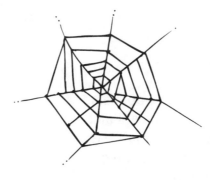 __ e __	 __ u __
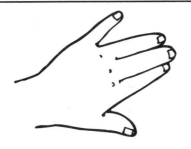 __ an __	 __ e __	 __ e __

Cluck! Cluck!

Skill: Short Vowels

Preparing the Center

1. Prepare an envelope following the directions on page 3.
   Cover—page 147
   Student Directions—page 149
   Sorting Pockets—pages 151–155
   Task Cards—pages 155–161
2. Reproduce a supply of the student activity sheet on page 163.
3. Place all center materials in the envelope.

Using the Center

In a Small Group

Place the short vowel sorting pockets (hens) in a row on a flat surface. Place the picture cards (eggs) in a small bag or box. One at a time, students take an egg from the bag, name the picture, and place it in the correct short vowel pocket. Continue until all eggs have been placed.

Independently

The student lines up the short vowel pockets. The student then names each picture and places it in the correct pocket. Finally, the student matches pictures to vowels on the activity sheet.

Self-Checking Key

Matching cards have the same short vowel on the back.

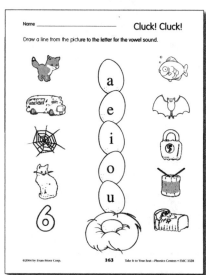

Cluck! Cluck!

148

Cluck! Cluck!

1. Put the hen pockets in a row.

2. Put each picture in the correct hen pocket.

3. Turn over the eggs to check your answers.

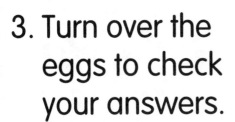

4. Complete the activity sheet.

Skill: Short Vowels

150

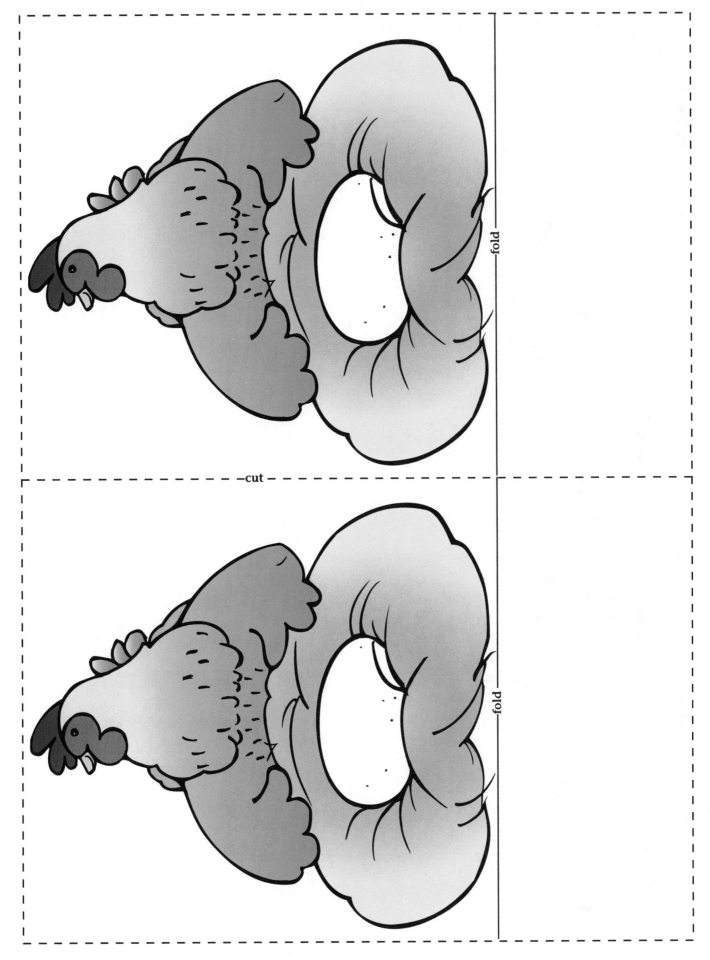

fold

—cut—

fold

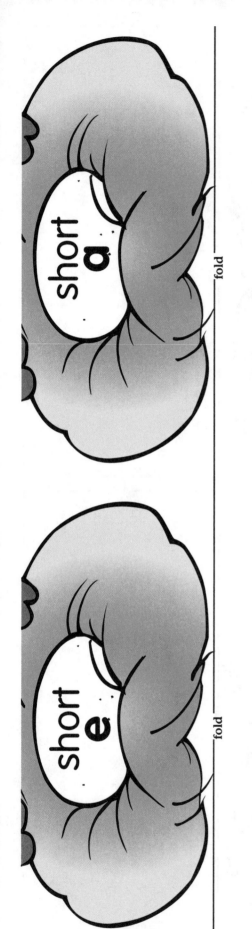

short **a**

fold

short **e**

fold

152

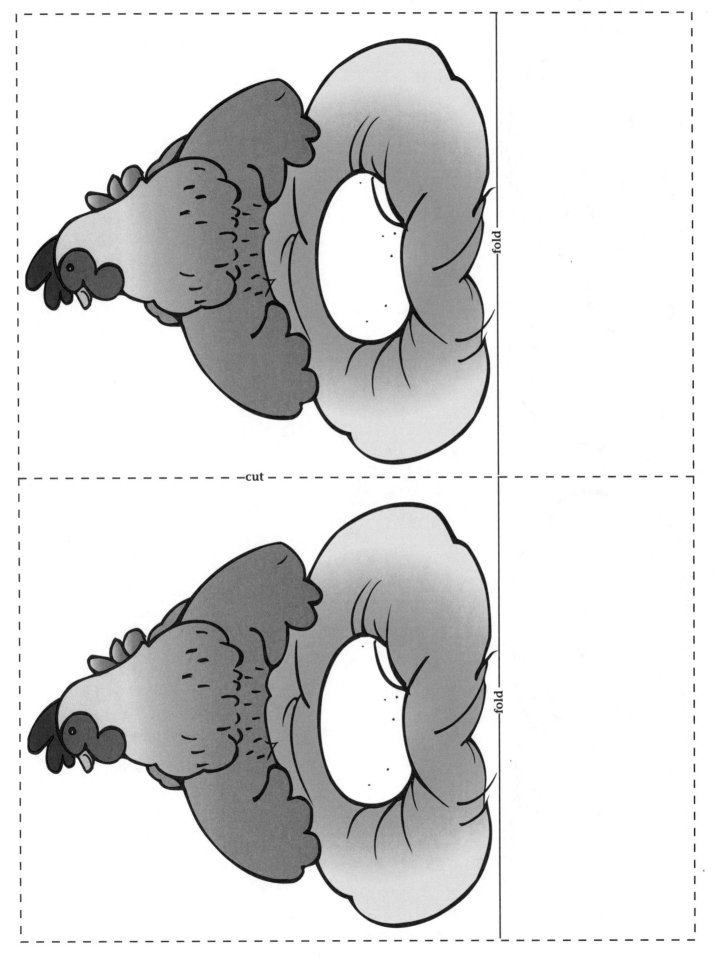

—cut—

fold

fold

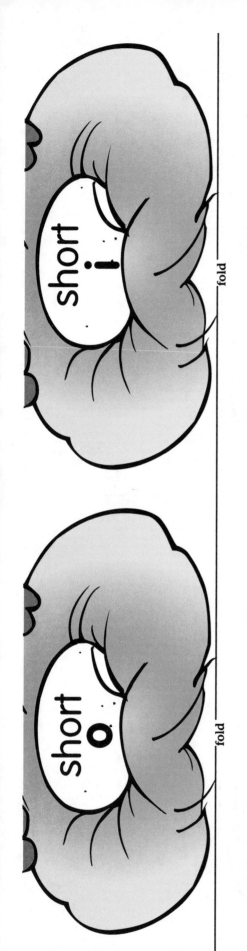

short i

fold

short o

fold

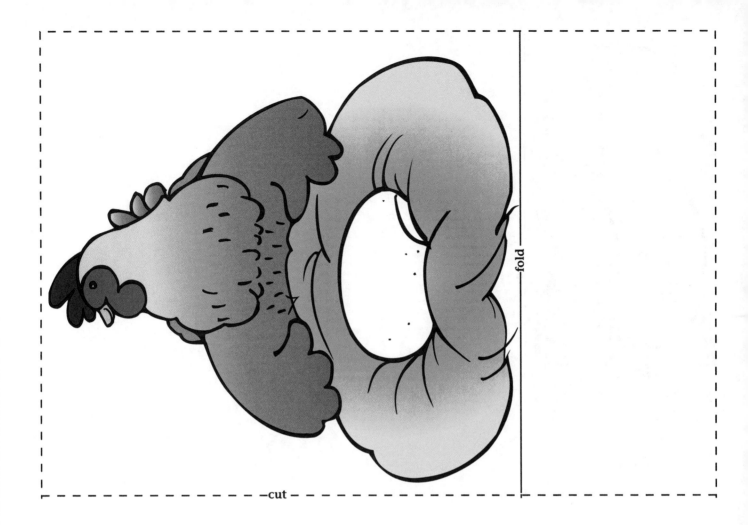

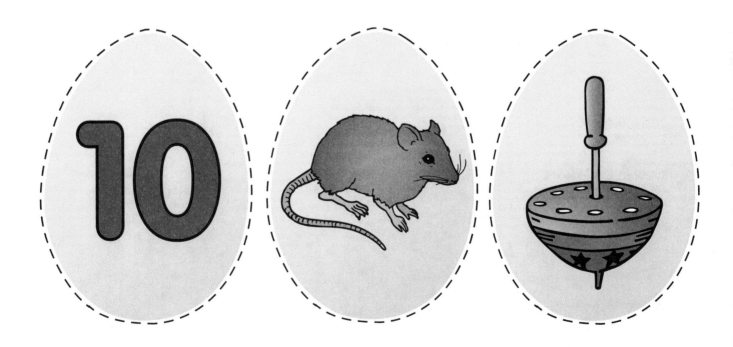

fold

short u

o

a

e

156

a

a

a

e

a

a

e

e

e

i

i

e

i

i

i

o

o

i

o

o

o

u

u

u

u

u

u

Name _____

Draw a line from the picture to the letter for the vowel sound.

What's Missing?

Skill: Short Vowels

Preparing the Center

1. Prepare an envelope following the directions on page 3.
   - Cover—page 165
   - Student Directions—page 167
   - Task Cards—pages 169–175
2. Reproduce a supply of the student activity sheet on page 177.
3. Place all center materials in the envelope.

Using the Center

In a Small Group

Lay the picture cards and the letter cards on a flat surface. Hold up a picture card. Students name the picture and identify the short vowel sound they hear. They find the letter card for that vowel sound and place it on the card. Continue the same process with the remaining picture cards.

Independently

The student uses the letter cards to place the short vowel sound on each picture card. Then the student writes the missing letters to complete each word on the activity sheet.

Self-Checking Key

The back of each short vowel picture card contains the completed word.

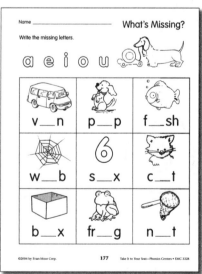

What's Missing?

166

What's Missing?

1. Name each picture.

2. Put the letter for the missing sound on the card.

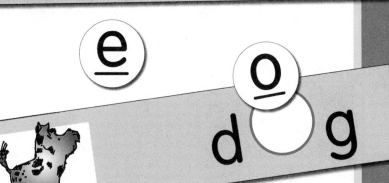

3. Turn over the picture cards to check your answers.

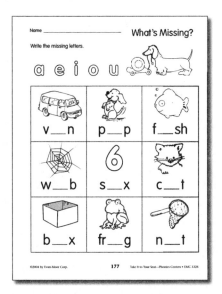

4. Complete the activity sheet.

Skill: Short Vowels

168

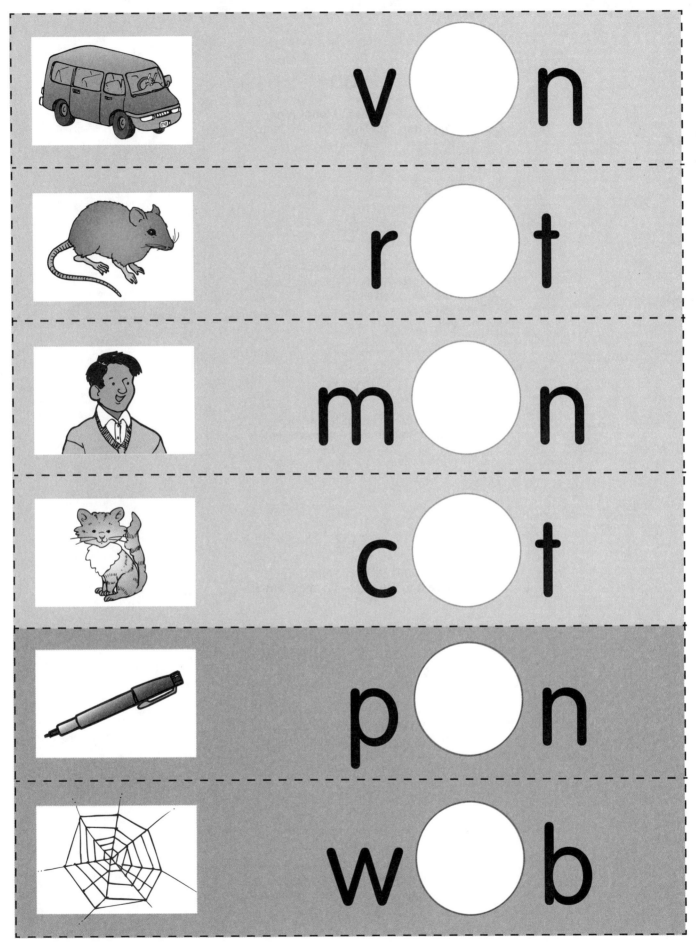

v ◯ n

r ◯ t

m ◯ n

c ◯ t

p ◯ n

w ◯ b

van

rat

man

cat

pen

web

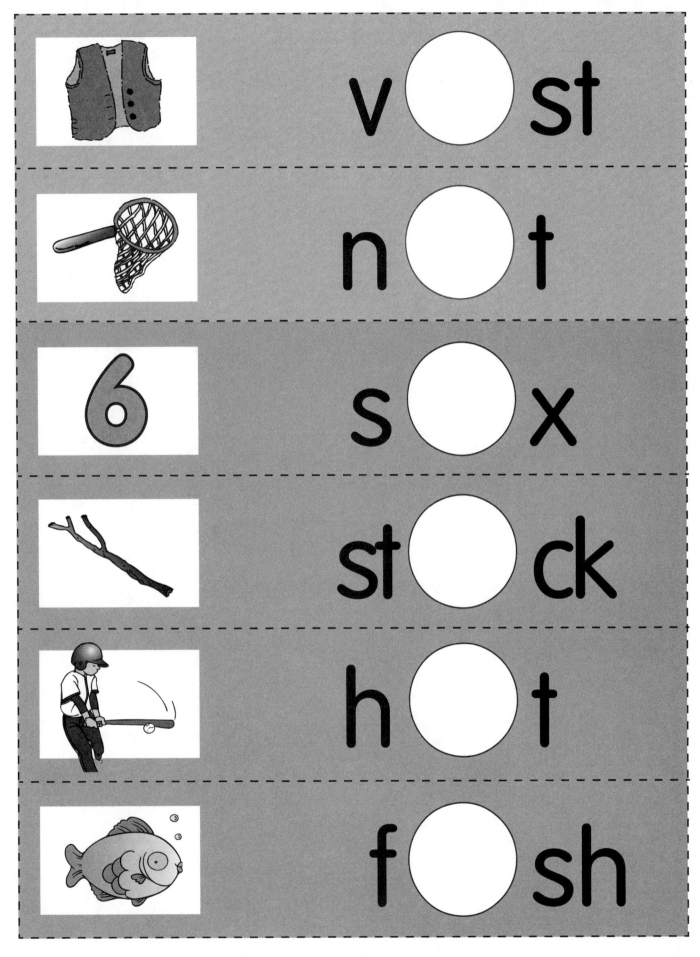

v◯st

n◯t

s◯x

st◯ck

h◯t

f◯sh

171

vest

net

six

stick

hit

fish

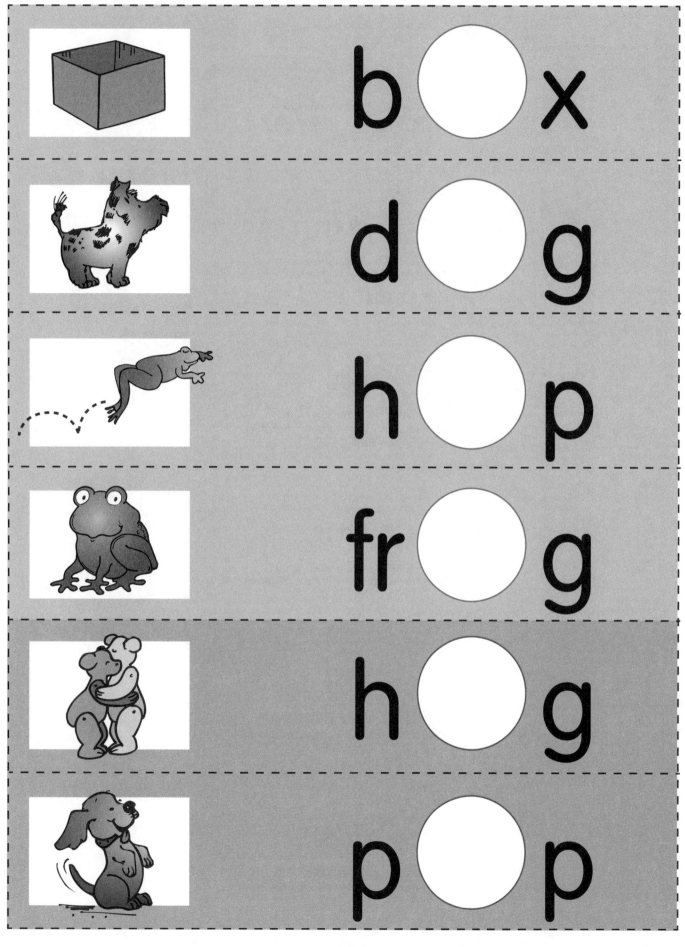

b◯x

d◯g

h◯p

fr◯g

h◯g

p◯p

173

box

dog

hop

frog

hug

pup

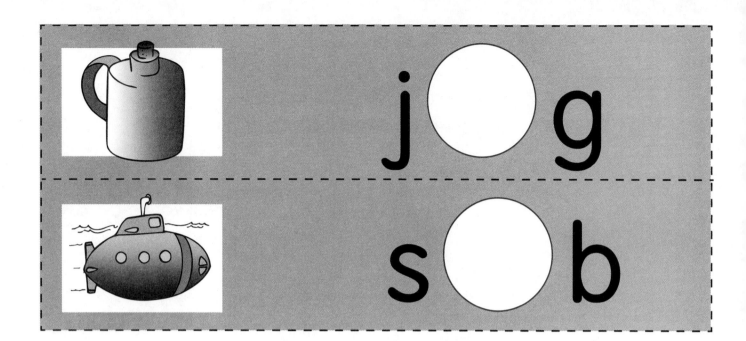

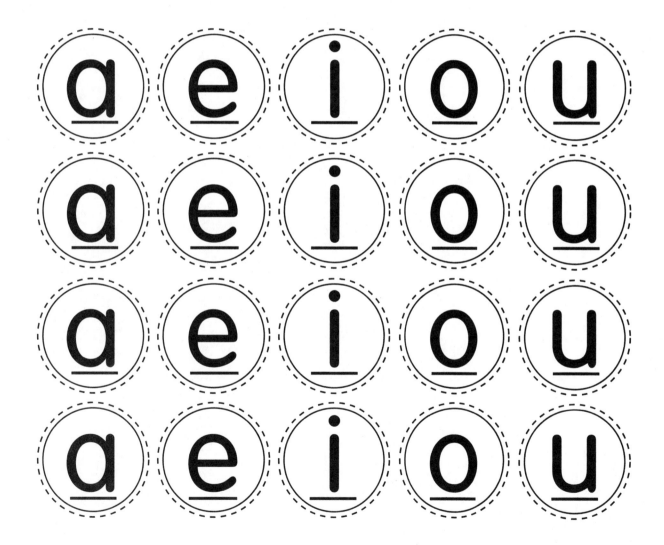

jug

sub

Name _____

Write the missing letters.

 a e i o u

v__n	p__p	f__sh

w__b	s__x	c__t
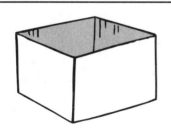		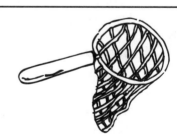
b__x	fr__g	n__t

177   Take It to Your Seat—Phonics Centers • EMC 3328

Count the Parts

Skill: Counting Syllables

Preparing the Center

1. Prepare an envelope following the directions on page 3.
   - Cover—page 179
   - Student Directions—page 181
   - Sorting Mats—page 183
   - Task Cards—pages 185–189
2. Reproduce a supply of the student activity sheet on page 191.
3. Place all center materials in the envelope.

Using the Center

In a Small Group

Place the sorting mats faceup on a flat surface. Place the picture cards in a small bag or box. One at a time, students draw a card and name the picture. The group decides how many parts the word contains. *Lion. Lion has two parts.* The student who drew the card places the picture on the correct sorting mat.

Students take turns drawing cards until the bag or box is empty.

Independently

The student sorts the picture cards by number of syllables, placing each picture on the correct mat. On the activity sheet, the student names each picture and circles the number of parts it contains.

Self-Checking Key

The number of syllables is indicated on the back of each card.

Count the Parts

clown
1

pop•corn
2

um•brel•la
3

179

180

Count the Parts

1. Say the name of each picture.

2. Listen for the number of parts in the word.

3. Put each card on the correct sorting mat.

4. Turn over the cards to check your answers.

5. Complete the activity sheet.

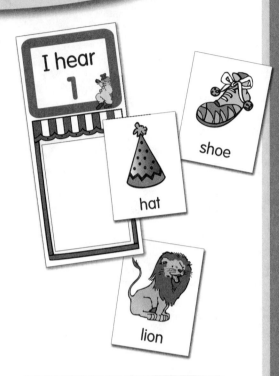

Skill: Counting Syllables

182

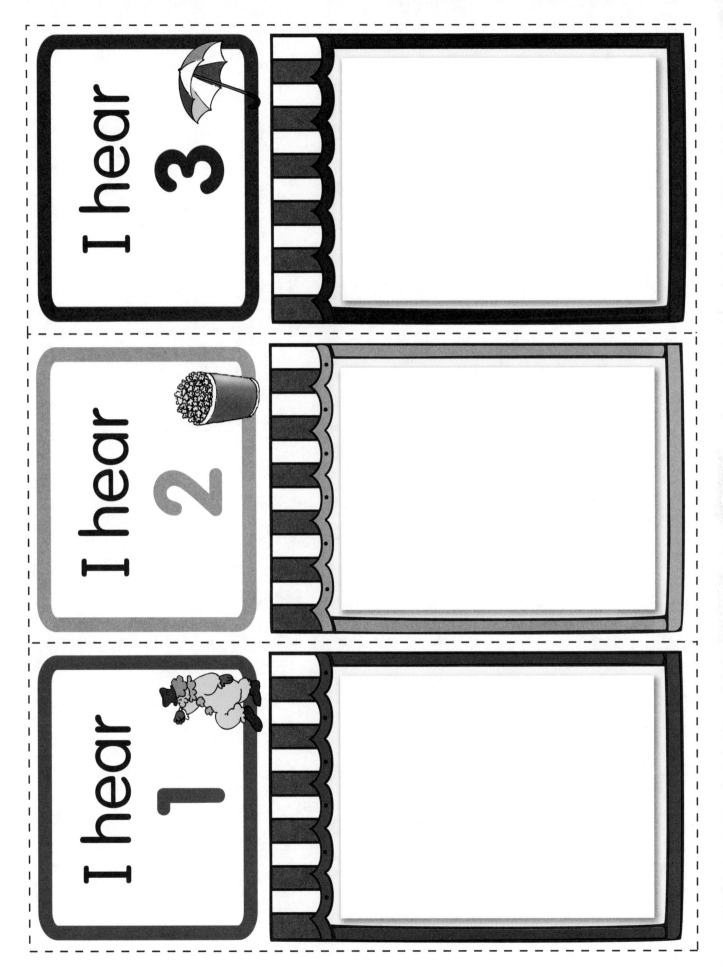

I hear
3

I hear
2

I hear
1

car

tent

flag

dog

hat

shoe

ball

bear

seal

1

1

1

1

1

1

1

1

1

monkey

wagon

baby

zebra

balloon

popcorn

lion

horses

ticket

elephant

acrobat

umbrella

ladybug

kangaroo

banana

magician

telephone

carousel

3

3

3

3

3

3

3

3

3

Name the picture. Circle the number of parts.

Count the Parts
1·2·3

1 2 3	1 2 3	1 2 3
1 2 3	1 2 3	1 2 3
1 2 3	1 2 3	1 2 3

ADMIT 1

Answer Key

Page 19 — Pair Them Up Puzzles
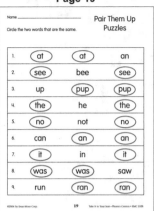

Page 33 — Rhymes Go Round

Page 47 — Ant Families
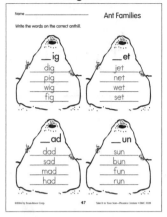

Page 61 — Cookie Sort
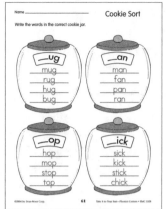

Page 75 — Bunch of Balloons
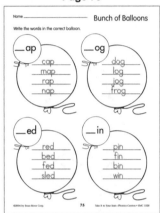

Page 91 — All Aboard the ABC Train

Page 101 — Beginning Sounds
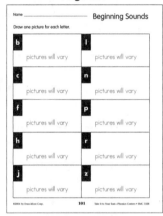

Page 117 — Flower Garden

Page 131 — What's at the End?

Page 145 — Make a Word

Page 163 — Cluck! Cluck!
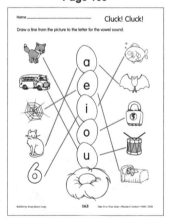

Page 177 — What's Missing?

Page 191 — Count the Parts